Reconstruction and the Aftermath of the Civil War

Lisa Colozza Cocca

CRABTREE
Publishing Company
www.crabtreebooks.com

UNDERSTANDING
THE CIVIL WAR

Author: Lisa Colozza Cocca
Publishing plan research and development:
   Sean Charlebois, Reagan Miller
   Crabtree Publishing Company
Editors: Mark Cheatham, Kirsten Holm, Lynn Peppas
Proofreader: Wendy Scavuzzo
Editorial director: Kathy Middleton
Production coordinator: Shivi Sharma
Creative director: Arka Roy Chaudhary
Design: Sandy Kent
Cover design: Samara Parent
Photo research: Iti Shrotriya
Maps: Paul Brinkdopke
Production coordinator: Margaret Amy Salter
Prepress technician: Margaret Amy Salter
Print coordinator: Katherine Berti

Written, developed, and produced by Planman Technologies

Photographs and Reproductions
Front cover: Library of Congree; Title Page (p. 1): Library of Congress; Table of Contents (p. 3): Chapter 1: The Granger Collection, New York, Chapter 2: Library of Congress, Chapter 3: Library of Congress, Chapter 4: Mary Evans Picture Library/Photolibrary, Chapter 5: The Granger Collection, New York. Chapter Opener image (pp. 5, 11, 19, 27, 35): Library of Congress
The Granger Collection: pp. 9, 33, 42; Library of Congress: pp. 4, 7, 10, 12, 13, 15, 17, 18, 21, 22, 26, 28, 29, 30, 37, 41, 43; Mary Evans Picture Library/Photolibrary: p. 31; North Wind: p. 32

Front cover: A joyous crowd greets President Abraham Lincoln in Richmond, Virginia, soon after the surrender of the city.
Back cover (background): A military map of the United States from 1862 shows forts and military posts.
Back cover (logo): A civil war era cannon stands in front of the flag from Fort Sumter.
Title page (top): Much of the South lay in ruins after the Civil War. This photo shows a burnt area of Richmond, Virginia, in 1865.
Title page (bottom): Reconstruction plans affected the lives of millions of former slaves, like this family in Richmond, Virginia.

Library and Archives Canada Cataloguing in Publication

Cocca, Lisa Colozza
      Reconstruction and the aftermath of the Civil War / Lisa Colozza Cocca.

(Understanding the Civil War)
Includes index.
Issued also in electronic formats.
ISBN 978-0-7787-5341-4 (bound).--ISBN 978-0-7787-5358-2 (pbk.)

      1. Reconstruction (U.S. history, 1865-1877)--Juvenile literature.
2. United States--History--Civil War, 1861-1865--Influence--Juvenile literature. 3. United States--History--1865-1898--Juvenile literature.
I. Title. II. Series: Understanding the Civil War

E668.C63 2011   j973.8   C2011-907488-5

Library of Congress Cataloging-in-Publication Data

Cocca, Lisa Colozza, 1957-
Reconstruction and the aftermath of the Civil War / Lisa Colozza Cocca.
      p. cm. -- (Understanding the Civil War)
  Includes index.
  ISBN 978-0-7787-5341-4 (reinforced library binding : alk. paper) --
ISBN 978-0-7787-5358-2 (pbk. : alk. paper) -- ISBN 978-1-4271-9940-9
(electronic pdf) -- ISBN 978-1-4271-9949-2 (electronic html)
 1. Reconstruction (U.S. history, 1865-1877)--Juvenile literature. 2. United
States--History--Civil War, 1861-1865--Influence--Juvenile literature. I.
Title.

 E668.C64 2011
 973.8--dc23
                                              2011045082

Crabtree Publishing Company

Printed in Canada/042016/BF20160217

www.crabtreebooks.com   1-800-387-7650

Published in Canada
Crabtree Publishing
616 Welland Ave.
St. Catharines, Ontario
L2M 5V6

Published in the United States
Crabtree Publishing
PMB 59051
350 Fifth Avenue, 59th Floor
New York, New York 10118

Published in the United Kingdom
Crabtree Publishing
Maritime House
Basin Road North, Hove
BN41 1WR

Published in Australia
Crabtree Publishing
3 Charles Street
Coburg North
VIC 3058

TABLE *of* CONTENTS

> *The attempt to place the white population under the domination of persons of color in the South has impaired, if not destroyed, the kindly relations that had previously existed between them; and . . . prevented that cooperation between the two races so essential to the success of industrial enterprise in the Southern States.*
>
> —President Andrew Johnson, December 25, 1868

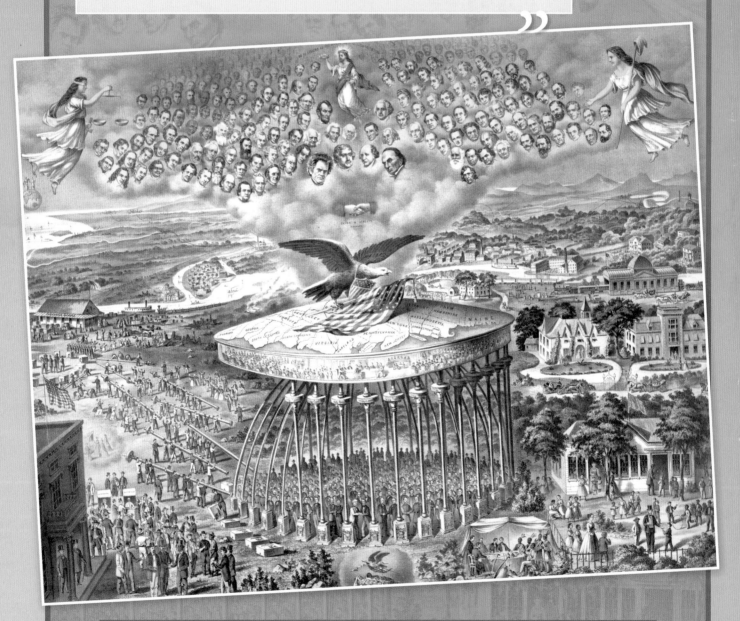

This print celebrates an idealized view of Reconstruction. The structure in the center represents the U.S. government. The collapsed pillars on the left are the Southern states which are being rebuilt by citizens. The figure of Jesus Christ in the center says, "Do unto others as you would have them do unto you."

Reconstruction

Reconstruction is the name given to the process of repairing the social, political, and physical effects of the Civil War. These efforts began before the Civil War ended. Reconstruction lasted 12 years, three times as long as the war lasted. President Lincoln's goals for Reconstruction were simple. He wanted to restore the nation and repair the damage caused by the war. Reaching those goals was not simple.

The Evolution of Reconstruction

At the onset of the war, Lincoln wanted to preserve the Union—with or without slavery. Over time, his views changed. He came to believe slavery **contradicted** the beliefs the nation was founded on.

Lincoln knew that many opposed the **emancipation**, or freeing, of the slaves. Southern Democrats believed owning slaves was their right. It was a part of their culture and their economy.

Lincoln faced trouble in the North, too. Before the Civil War, in 1854, many Northern Whigs had left their party. They formed the Republican Party. The new party believed the country needed to end slavery. Lincoln knew, however, that most Northerners did not agree with the Republicans. He knew he had to find a way to unite Americans behind his goals. He needed a plan to preserve the Union and end slavery.

Major Events

1862

March
Law passed stopping the army from returning runaway slaves

April
District of Columbia Emancipation Act

July
Second Confiscation Act

1863

January
Final Emancipation Proclamation

December
Proclamation of Amnesty and Reconstruction

...we went to bed one night old fashioned, conservative, Compromise Union Whigs and waked up stark mad Abolitionists.

—Amos A. Lawrence, textile magnate

Emancipation

The road to emancipation was a long and bumpy one. The South decided to leave the Union to avoid being forced to free its slaves. Many in the North did not accept this idea. Northern Democrats had been divided on how to solve the secession problem. One group believed war was the only answer. The other thought peace talks would solve the problem. Emancipation brought these two sides together. They both opposed freeing the slaves.

Lincoln faced difficulties even within his own party. Radical Republicans wanted freedom and equal rights for the slaves. Moderate and Conservative Republicans did not agree. They were worried about the effects of emancipation. They knew it would change life in the North as well as in the South. Many were not ready to see formerly enslaved people as their equals.

One Step at a Time

Lincoln realized emancipation would have to come in small steps. The government began by taking these actions:

- March 1862: Congress passed an article of war. It **prohibited** the army from returning escaped slaves to their masters.
- April 19, 1862: Congress passed the District of Columbia Emancipation Act. This ended slavery in the nation's capital. Owners were repaid up to $300 for each slave that was freed.
- July 17, 1862: Congress passed the Second Confiscation Act. It freed the slaves who lived in Union-occupied territories or who escaped to Union lines. This act only covered slaves belonging to masters who were disloyal to the Union.

> *I do order and declare that all persons held as slaves within said designated states, and parts of states, are, and henceforward shall be free; and that the Executive government of the United States, including the military and naval authorities thereof, will recognize and maintain the freedom of said persons.*
>
> —President Abraham Lincoln, "Final Emancipation Proclamation," January 1, 1863

The Emancipation Proclamation

Lincoln signed the Emancipation Proclamation on January 1, 1863. It ended slavery in areas that were fighting against the Union. At first, this act freed few people. It only covered slavery in places where the Union had no control. It did not free slaves in the parts of the South the Union already controlled. It did not end slavery in the border states, which remained in the Union where slavery was legal. Despite this, it was a very important document. It changed the course of the war. The North was no longer fighting only to save the Union. Now it was also fighting to end slavery.

The World Reacts

The Emancipation Proclamation received mixed reviews both at home and abroad. Abolitionists said it did not go far enough. They wanted freedom for slaves in every state. Northern Democrats saw it as an end to their own safety, job security, and civil rights. They reacted to it with violence and riots.

This print celebrates the emancipation of Southern slaves. It contrasts life under slavery (left) with a life of freedom (right and center). A picture of Abraham Lincoln appears at the bottom of the print.

Across the ocean, the British also had mixed reactions. Many felt the Proclamation was too weak to be helpful. Others saw it as a step in the right direction. In the end, the Proclamation changed the British position on the war. Britain had not supported the North's stand on preserving the Union. However, now that the North was also fighting against slavery, it sided with the North.

Lincoln's Reconstruction Plan

Lincoln knew the country needed a plan for recovery even before the war ended. There were over three million slaves in the country. Once they were freed, they would need help finding homes and jobs. The question of **social equality**, or equal rights and opportunities for African Americans and whites, had to be addressed. Those were only two of the many problems the Union faced.

The country needed a clear plan for dealing with the rebellious states. The Union had to figure out how to deal with citizens of states that had seceded and the punishment of Confederate leaders. They also had to plan how to rebuild the South.

THE EMANCIPATION PROCLAMATION

The Emancipation Proclamation enabled African Americans to join the army. In all, 180,000 African Americans fought for the Union. This arrangement highlighted the promise and the problems of abolition.

The African-American soldiers learned how to read and write. They received medical care and a paycheck. They served, however, in **segregated** units. They were under the command of white officers. Although they were paid, they received less than the white soldiers. Despite this inequality, 26 African-American soldiers earned the Congressional Medal of Honor.

A Second Proclamation

Almost a year passed after the Emancipation Proclamation before Lincoln took the next major step. On December 8, 1863, he announced his Proclamation of Amnesty and Reconstruction. **Amnesty** is the act of forgiving a group of people. Lincoln's plan offered amnesty to most Confederates.

> *We are like whalers who have been on a long chase. We have at last got the harpoon into the monster, but we must look now how we steer, or with one flop of his tail he will send us all into eternity.*
>
> —President Abraham Lincoln, in conversation to a friend, January 1863

To receive amnesty, a person had to do several things. First, he had to take an oath of future loyalty to the United States and its laws. Second, he had to promise to accept abolition. If he did these things, there would be no punishment. This offer was not open to everyone. High ranking officers in the Confederate Army or high ranking Confederate public leaders could not get amnesty.

Lincoln believed secession was against the law. He did not accept the idea that states could choose to leave the Union. In his eyes, the states were still a part of the country. They did not need rules to return to statehood in the Union because they had never legally left. He thought all that was needed was to put Union leaders in control of the Confederate states.

This 1865 political cartoon oversimplifies Lincoln's huge task of repairing the Union. Lincoln, the "railsplitter" (right) and his vice-president Andrew Johnson (the tailor) attempt to stitch up the Union with a needle and thread.

Radical Opposition

When Lincoln introduced this Reconstruction plan, it was met with opposition. The Radical Republicans believed the Confederate states had given up their right to statehood when they seceded. The Radicals felt these states were now provinces or territories of the Union. As such, they had no say in laws or leadership.

The Radicals also disagreed with Lincoln on amnesty. They believed giving former rebels the full rights of citizenship meant the social structure of the South would remain the same. If the land remained with the wealthy white owners, the freed slaves would have little chance of bettering their lives. Without land or a job, the slaves would be forced to work for their former owners under the same old conditions.

The Radicals did agree with one point in Lincoln's plan. They agreed that Union loyalists should govern the Southern states. They thought the best way to achieve that was to give the freed slaves the right to vote.

 **What Do You Know!**

The "Battle Hymn of the Republic" was written by Julia Ward Howe, a white abolitionist. It is sung to the melody of a popular soldiers' tune, "John Brown's body lies a-mouldering in the grave." Howe thought the tune should be paired with more positive lyrics.

A Moderate View

The Radical Republicans held extreme views for the time. Moderate Republicans took more of a middle-of-the-road approach. They agreed that Unionists should be in charge of the Southern states. They did not, however, support the idea of voting rights for the freed slaves. Only six Northern states allowed African-American men to vote. Strong feelings of white **supremacy** existed in both the North and South. The Moderates, as well as the president, worried that giving freed slaves the vote would turn people away from the cause.

Much of the South lay in ruins after the Civil War. This photo shows a burnt area of Richmond, Virginia, in 1865.

Congress Wants Control

Lincoln knew that many of the conflicts over his plan were, in part, a struggle for control with Congress. Lincoln had been able to take steps toward Reconstruction because the Constitution gave him extra powers during wartime. Congress wanted to claim power over Reconstruction.

If secession meant the states had lost their statehood and were territories, then Congress would control them. The Constitution gives Congress the power to govern territories. It also gives Congress the power to admit new states. If Lincoln's approach were adopted, the states would remain states. In that case, the Constitution gave the power to the **executive branch**. Then the president had the authority to grant amnesty and to set the terms for restoring the states to their full status.

Moving Ahead

Lincoln was flexible about his Reconstruction plan. He knew he needed a good deal of support to bring the war to an end and to reunite the Union. The bad feelings among Americans were growing. The battles left behind a path of destruction. Lincoln understood that his plan answered only some of the questions about Reconstruction. He knew it created many new ones. Lincoln also knew, though, that he would use the powers the Constitution gave him. He would do all he could to reunite and rebuild the country.

Lincoln's Ten Percent Plan

There was no shortage of plans to put the fractured nation back together, even before the war was over. Each plan created different paths for the Southern states to become a part of the United States again. Different groups proposed competing plans. Choosing the best plan to reconstruct the nation became a struggle.

Major Events

1863

December
Proclamation of Amnesty and Reconstruction

1864

February
Louisiana holds elections for new state leaders

July
Wade-Davis Bill goes to Congress

Presidential Reconstruction

In December 1863, President Lincoln put forward his Amnesty and Reconstruction Plan, called the Ten Percent Plan. It laid out how state governments would be reestablished. This plan paved the way for rebellious states to return to the Union.

Lincoln wanted it to be easy for these states to rejoin the Union. He believed a plan of forgiveness would bring a quicker end to the war.

The plan set a few conditions for readmission to the Union with all the rights other states had. First, a certain number of white males in the state had to take an oath of loyalty to the Union. This number had to equal at least ten percent of the people who voted in 1860 in the state. If they met that number, the voters could set up a new state government. That government would then write a new state constitution that declared slavery was ended forever in that state. The Ten Percent Plan let states adopt temporary measures to deal with the problems resulting from freeing the slaves, such as finding jobs, housing, and land for freedmen.

> *The Ten Percent Plan will be 'a rallying point— a plan of action.'*
> —Abraham Lincoln, 1863

Rebuilding the States

The Union was gaining ground. It now controlled large parts of rebel states, including most of Tennessee and parts of Louisiana, Arkansas, Mississippi, and Virginia. The Ten Percent Plan was immediately in effect in these areas.

Temporary Leaders

Lincoln appointed temporary military governors to these occupied areas (see table below). Lincoln had specific goals for these leaders. One was to put new loyal governments in place. The state leaders had to accept the authority of the federal government. The military governor encouraged citizens to take the oath of loyalty. He enforced the proclamations—including ending slavery. Once he met these goals, the military governor was no longer needed.

A Test Case

Louisiana was the perfect test case for Lincoln's Ten Percent Plan. New Orleans was the largest city in the Deep South. Union forces took control of the city in April 1862. Most of the city's population was white. Many people had been born in the North or abroad. They worked as bankers, lawyers, doctors, and businessmen.

New Orleans also had the largest community of free African Americans in the Deep South. Most were of mixed race. They did not have the right to vote, but they did have many other civil rights. They could travel freely. They could testify against whites in court, and they could own land. Many of them were skilled craftsmen. They worked as masons, carpenters, shoemakers, and cigar makers. Their children attended school.

People After the War

John Smith Phelps

Colonel Phelps was the Civil War military governor of Arkansas. A Democrat, Phelps had previously served as a congressman for Missouri and as a regiment leader for the Union Army. His wife, Mary, is believed to be the first female Union nurse. Phelps made waves when he complained about the poor conditions African-American soldiers were living in within Arkansas. He criticized the Union army for profiting from the state's cotton crops. He left office on July 9, 1863.

Reconstruction Military Districts	
State	*Military Governor*
Louisiana	George F. Shepley
Tennessee	Andrew Johnson
Arkansas	Colonel John S. Phelps
Mississippi	Edward Ord
Virginia	John Potts Slough

The Union also took control of some areas with sugar and cotton plantations. The owners had been Whigs and **Conditional Unionists**. Conditional Unionists were Southern people who felt strong ties to the Union but left because of a particular issue. They were quick to take the oath of allegiance.

Within this population, it was easy to achieve the ten percent needed to take the oath and accept abolition.

President
Abraham Lincoln

Elections

George F. Shepley, a Radical Republican, was military governor of Louisiana. Nathaniel Banks was the Republican commander of occupying forces. Both men were ready to help with Reconstruction. The occupied areas of Louisiana included two main groups of people. One group was plantation owners who had been slow to accept emancipation. They wanted to elect a new government under Louisiana's old constitution. A second group, the Free State General Committee, included people who had not wanted to secede from the Union. Many had refused to help the Confederacy. They wanted to write a new constitution and abolish slavery. They wanted to elect new leaders so they could rejoin the Union.

Banks worried about some of the Free State General Committee's ideas. They wanted African Americans to have the right to vote, within limits. Banks believed this idea was too radical for most whites to accept. He decided to break the group into Conservative, Moderate, and Radical sections. Each section had their own candidates. An election was held on February 22, 1864. The Moderate candidates received more votes than the Conservatives and Radicals combined.

A Constitutional Convention

Following the election, Louisiana held its convention. New Orleans was named the state capital. The constitution set a minimum wage and a maximum workday. It established free public education. It abolished slavery, but it did not give the freed slaves the right to vote.

> *...there could be no middle ground in a revolution. It must work a radical change in society; such had been the history of every great revolution.*
>
> —Thomas J. Durrant, leader of the Free State General Committee

...the history of the world shows that revolutions which are not controlled, and held within reasonable limits, produce counter revolutions.

—Nathaniel Banks, in a letter to President Lincoln

Strengths and Weaknesses

Testing the Ten Percent Plan in Louisiana and in the other four Union occupied areas made the strengths and weaknesses of the plan clear. One of the greatest strengths of the plan was that it was simple. The occupied areas had to do little to move from rebel to loyal status. They did not need a majority to agree to the plan. They only needed ten percent of the voting population to take the oath. Since in some places the Union occupied only about half of the state, this meant a very small percentage of the population spoke for the state. This made the move back into the Union quick and easy. Since there were no harsh punishments for the majority of the citizens, return was more appealing.

In addition, the Ten Percent Plan laid out a clear path for replacing the current state governments with new governments loyal to the Union. This assured the citizens that Lincoln wanted them to once again have a say in the Union. The plan allowed the new governments to maintain their old laws, boundaries, and constitution. The only condition was that these things had to be in agreement with the other provisions of the amnesty proclamation.

The plan provided that these states would have the full rights and privileges of all loyal states. This included protection from **domestic** or foreign forces. This also meant that trade would be open again to these states.

The greatest weakness of the plan was what it did not include. Although it gave enslaved people in these areas freedom, it fell short of giving them a voice in their government.

Reconstruction plans affected the lives of millions of former slaves like this family in Richmond, Virginia.

Free and Then What?

The Ten Percent Plan required the rebel states to abolish slavery to regain their loyal state status. It did little to help the freed slaves adapt to their new life. Slavery had provided them with jobs and homes. As freedmen, they were jobless and homeless.

One option available to the freedmen was to join the Union Army. The Emancipation Proclamation had opened the doors to escaped slaves to join the army. Many slaves saw service as a way to freedom. Now already freed men were drawn to service. The army gave

> *Do we not cover the same space of ground? Do we not take up the same length of ground in a grave-yard that others do?*
>
> —Edward D. Washington, Union private, 54th Colored Regiment of the Massachusetts Volunteers, in a letter, March 13

the men food, shelter, and medical care. It gave them a basic education and a paycheck. It did not give them equality. African-American soldiers were paid less and often lived in extremely poor conditions.

For many former slaves, though, serving in the Union forces was an opportunity. Many African-American political leaders first served as soldiers, including 41 delegates to state constitutional conventions and three lieutenant governors. Several former African-American soldiers even earned a place in the federal government as congressmen.

The prejudice that freed slaves faced in civilian life was even greater than what they faced in the army. Many plantation owners who had signed oaths did so for the trade protection they provided, not because they supported abolition.

The steps the government took reinforced the lower status of African Americans, even though that was not intended. On January 29, 1863, just weeks after the Emancipation Proclamation, Nathaniel Banks issued an order. It said plantation owners could hire the freed slaves to work for $3 a month or 5% of the year's crop. In return, landowners had to provide "just treatment, healthy rations, comfortable clothing, quarters, fuel, medical attendance, and instruction for children."

The army forced the freed slaves to sign yearly contracts with the landowners. The freedmen were allowed only limited travel within a pass system. To the African Americans forced into this agreement, free labor did not seem much different than slavery. In 1864, Banks increased the wages. He let the freedmen choose who they wanted to work for and forced the landowners to give the workers a garden plot.

The one thing the freed slaves were happy with was the order to open schools. Both Banks' order and Lincoln's Ten Percent Plan required areas to provide a free public education to the freed people. By October 1864, Louisiana had 78 new schools with 7,900 students and 125 teachers.

> *Prejudice against the colored people is exhibited continually... a prejudice bitter and vulgar.*
>
> —Salmon P. Chase, Secretary of the Treasury, on conditions of the freed slaves in Louisiana

"*I barely suggest for your private consideration, whether some of the colored people not be let in—as for instance, the very intelligent, and especially those who have fought gallantly in our ranks… But this is only a suggestion, not to the public, but to you alone.*"

—Abraham Lincoln in a letter to Louisiana Governor Michael Hahn, March 13, 1864

The Debate Continues

One clause in the Ten Percent Plan called for a "republican form of government" in the former rebel states. This opened Reconstruction plans to input from the president and Congress. Lincoln saw his plan as a beginning, not an end. He knew it would face **opposition**.

Thaddeus Stevens was one person who opposed the plan. Stevens was a Radical Republican who believed in equality for all men. He had been fighting for **suffrage**, or the right to vote, for African Americans since 1838. Stevens thought the emancipation and amnesty proclamations did not do enough for the African Americans. He also opposed the forgiving nature of the Ten Percent Plan. Stevens believed the basic foundations of the Confederate states had to be broken down and replaced. He thought if their old institutions were allowed to survive, then the African Americans would see no improvement in their lives.

Unlike Lincoln, Stevens believed the states no longer existed. He believed them to be conquered territories. As such, they were subject to the will of their conquerors—the Union.

Stevens' ideas were extreme even among other Radicals. Charles Sumner was a Republican Senator from Massachusetts. He, too, was a member of the Radicals. Sumner had long supported freedom for the slaves. He, like Stevens, thought Lincoln's proclamations did not go far enough. His opinion on the seceded states, however, was somewhere

Thaddeus Stevens was a Radical Republican who opposed Lincoln's Ten Percent Plan.

> *Give me the money that has been spent in war and I will clothe every man, woman, and child … I will build a schoolhouse in every valley over the whole earth. I will crown every hillside with a place of worship consecrated [dedicated] to peace.*
>
> —Charles Sumner, Radical Republican, after the Civil War

Charles Sumner, a U.S. senator from Massachusetts, was a leading Radical Republican.

between Lincoln and Stevens. Sumner agreed with Lincoln that the Union was **indestructible**. The states had not left the Union. He said that by attempting to leave the Union, they had committed "state suicide." In so doing, they gave up their rights as states. They were now territories.

A growing number of Republicans supported the idea of suffrage for African-American males. Even Lincoln was starting to lean toward limited African-American suffrage. Sumner's idea about the territories also had strong support. Declaring the states to be territories would greatly increase the control of Congress over Reconstruction. The process of Reconstruction was becoming a war within the war. Two Radical Republicans, Senator Benjamin Wade and Representative Henry Davis, were about to strike the next blow.

The Wade-Davis Bill

I n the North, both Republicans and Democrats were unhappy with Lincoln's plan. They believed it was too easy and forgiving. They feared it gave too much power to the states. Confederates might sign the oath and then return to their old ways. Arguments between **Ironclad Unionists** and former rebels fueled the fire. Ironclad Unionists were people in the South who had never supported the Confederacy.

Policies in Louisiana

Politicians in the North worried about what was happening in Louisiana. They pointed to the policies in place there. One required former slaves to have a pass to leave the plantation. Another forced freedmen to work for their former owners. They ignored the fact that Nathaniel Banks set these policies. Instead, they pointed a finger at the new state government that was forming.

> *The Constitution declares the abolition of Slavery, prohibits involuntary servitude except for crime. . . It makes all men equal before the law.*
>
> —Nathaniel Banks describing the results of the Louisiana State Constitutional Convention October 1, 1864

Major Events

1864

June 15
Thirteenth Amendment fails

July 2
Wade-Davis Bill passes in Congress

July 8
Lincoln pocket vetoes Wade-Davis Bill

August 5
Wade-Davis Manifesto

September
Louisiana State Constitution

November 8
Lincoln reelected

December 6
Lincoln sends Message of Compromise

The Franchise

The Radical Republicans continued to push to **franchise** the African-American population. This would give African Americans the full rights of citizenship. In particular, it would give the vote to African-American men.

At the same time, Radical Republicans wanted to **disenfranchise** former rebels. They believed by taking away their vote and giving African Americans the vote, Republicans would gain a stronghold in the South.

A Constitutional Amendment

> *"Neither slavery nor involuntary servitude... shall exist within the United States, or any place subject to their jurisdiction."*
>
> —The Thirteenth Amendment to the Constitution

Lincoln could not calm his party's fears. Republicans looked for a way to end any chance of the South returning to slavery. The answer came in the form of a **constitutional amendment**. In 1864, Republicans attempted to pass the Thirteenth Amendment. It would abolish slavery throughout the country.

The Republicans were united in support of the amendment. On this issue, Lincoln agreed with his party. In the Senate, a two-thirds majority was needed to pass an amendment. The Republicans had an easy time rounding up the needed votes. The Senate quickly passed the amendment.

The House of Representatives was a different matter. In the 1862 House elections, Democrats had gained a number of seats. When the amendment came up for vote in the House, it lost by 13 votes. The attempt to pass the Thirteenth Amendment was not successful.

The Wade-Davis Bill

The defeat of the amendment increased Republicans' worries. It pushed the Radicals to come up with a plan of their own for Reconstruction. Benjamin Wade was a senator from Ohio. He had helped establish the Republican Party there and was respected in the North. He had a history as an opponent of slavery. Wade was also the chairman of the Senate's

Special Committee on the Conduct of the War. He had advised Lincoln to end the Civil War through battle rather than through peace talks.

Henry Winter Davis was a member of the House of Representatives. The Maryland Republican shared Wade's radical views. The two men worked together to create the Wade-Davis Bill of 1864. The bill presented their plan for Reconstruction.

Senator Benjamin Wade, U.S. senator and co-sponsor of the Wade-Davis Bill of 1864

Requiring More From the South

The plan was different from Lincoln's plan on two main points. Lincoln's plan required at least ten percent of the voting population to take the loyalty oath. The Wade-Davis plan required at least 50 percent of the voters in the state to take the oath.

The other main difference was in the oath. Under Lincoln's plan, anyone wishing to rejoin the Union had to swear to uphold the authority of the federal government and to abide by its laws and proclamations, including emancipation. The Wade-Davis plan demanded a second, much more limiting oath. Known as the Ironclad Oath, it required a person to swear that he had never helped the Confederacy.

The Wade-Davis plan required a state constitutional convention to take place. Only then could any state elections be held. Only men who took the Ironclad Oath could vote for a convention.

> *I, _____, do solemnly swear, in presence of Almighty God, that I will henceforth faithfully support, protect, and defend the Constitution of the United States and the Union of the States thereunder; and that I will, in like manner, abide by and faithfully support all acts of congress passed during the existing rebellion with reference to slaves, so long and so far as not repealed, modified, or held void by congress, or by decision of the supreme court; and that I will, in like manner, abide by and faithfully support all proclamations of the President made during the existing rebellion having reference to slaves, so long and so far as not modified or declared void by decision of the supreme court. So help me God.*
>
> —Oath of Loyalty, The Proclamation of Amnesty and Reconstruction

Henry W. Davis, co-sponsor of the Wade-Davis Bill of 1864.

Quite simply, it would be almost impossible to get 50 percent of white men from a Southern state to take the Ironclad Oath. This would postpone, or delay, Reconstruction.

African-American Suffrage

The Wade-Davis bill also required equality for African Americans, except when it came to voting. The original bill had included the right of African Americans to vote. However, Wade was concerned the bill would not pass with this included, so he removed it. Davis made another change to the bill. He added a **preamble**, or introductory statement. In it, he referred to the Confederate states as the "public enemy." His words represented the feelings of many Northern Republicans.

On May 4, 1864, the bill passed in the House of Representatives. On July 3rd, it was passed by the Senate without any further changes. Then it was in the hands of the president.

Lincoln Uses the Veto

Lincoln had no intention of passing the bill. He believed the Ten Percent Plan was working in Louisiana. The state had easily met the quota. The people had elected officials. They were working on a state constitution that pleased Lincoln. The president feared the Wade-Davis plan would undo this work. Congress had already voted not to recognize the former rebel states' representatives in the House and Senate.

> *Now, therefore, I, Abraham Lincoln, President of the United States, do proclaim, declare, and make known, that, while I am... unprepared, by a formal approval of this Bill . . . but am at the same time, sincerely hoping and expecting that a constitutional amendment, abolishing slavery throughout the nation, may be adopted...*
>
> Abraham Lincoln, Proclamation on the Wade-Davis Bill, July 8, 1864

Lincoln also saw the Wade-Davis Bill as a way to **postpone** Reconstruction until after the war was over. Lincoln believed the Union needed to start Reconstruction right away. He believed that by establishing new state governments in the South he was weakening the Confederacy. He thought this would help end the war faster and with a Union victory.

The U.S. Constitution outlines how a bill becomes a law. First, a bill has to pass through both houses of Congress. The Wade-Davis Bill did that. Next, it has to be approved by the president. Once a bill passes through Congress, the president has ten days to either approve it or veto it. If the president does neither, then the bill automatically becomes a law.

There is an exception to those rules. Sometimes a bill passes through Congress less than ten days before the end of a congressional session. In that case, the president can stop it from becoming a law by simply ignoring, or "pocketing" the bill.

Lincoln chose to **pocket veto** the bill. He said Congress could not abolish slavery with a federal law. He said the bill would make secession legal. Lincoln said that the only way Congress could accomplish its goal was to pass an amendment. He told Congress to get back to work on passing the Thirteenth Amendment to the Constitution.

> "
> *The rash and fatal act of the President was a blow at the friends of his Administration, at the rights of humanity, and at the principles of Republican Government.*
>
> —Wade-Davis Manifesto, August 5, 1864
> "

The Wade-Davis Manifesto

Wade and Davis were furious. Congress was not in session. That meant they had no way to respond through the government to the veto. This did not stop them. They wrote a **manifesto**, or a public statement of their thoughts and motives. They had their manifesto published in the newspaper.

Wade and Davis had harsh words for the president. They accused him of overstepping his powers. They said the president was motivated by politics. Lincoln was running for reelection. Wade and Davis believed that if given the chance to vote, all of the former rebels would vote for Lincoln.

People in the War

Jean-Charles Houzeau

Houzeau became editor of the *New Orleans Tribune* in November 1864. He expanded the readership of the paper to include Northern Republicans. The paper spread a message of black suffrage and equality before the law. It pushed for the **desegregation** of the Louisiana schools and streetcars. It supported giving plots of land to the freedmen.

Houzeau, through the paper, influenced the opinions of the Northern Republicans.

The 1864 Nomination

Wade and Davis, however, were also motivated by politics. The election year had exposed the deep cracks that had formed within the Republican Party. Lincoln's Reconstruction plan was unpopular. The Confederacy seemed to be fighting with renewed strength. Despair over the war was spreading throughout the Union. Many wondered if the Union could win.

The Republican Convention

Lincoln was not guaranteed his party's nomination for reelection. In fact, no president had been reelected since 1840. Many sections of his party were considering other nominees. One of the suggestions was Salmon P. Chase, a good friend of Wade.

In the second week of June, the Republicans held their convention. They changed the name to the National Union Convention. They hoped this would draw in some War Democrats and some Southern Unionists. The party platform included a push to get the Thirteenth Amendment passed. It also backed Lincoln's outlook of unconditional surrender of the rebel states.

The Republicans rallied around these causes. They avoided the topic of Reconstruction. In the end, they nominated Lincoln for a second term. Many of the Radicals were not happy with this choice. Wade and Davis were among them. They hoped their manifesto, written two months after Lincoln's nomination, would change minds. They hoped it would encourage Republicans to run a different candidate.

> *...excellent, better for the poor black man than we have in Illinois.*
>
> —Abraham Lincoln, on the Louisiana State Constitution

The Louisiana Constitution

Louisiana **ratified** its state constitution in September 1864. The end result proved Congress wrong. The constitution ended slavery in the state. It called for public schools for all children. It opened the army to African Americans and promised equal rights in the courts. It did not give African Americans the right to vote. African Americans could fight for their government, but they would not have a voice in it.

> *We cannot have free government without elections; and if the rebellion could force us to forego, or postpone a national election, it might fairly claim to have already conquered and ruined us.*
>
> —Abraham Lincoln, November 10, 1864

The Election of 1864

In the months before the election, Lincoln was discouraged about the war. He began to feel sure his opponent George McClellan would win the presidential election. McClellan was a Democrat who had served as the general-in-chief of the Union Army. After many problems, the president had removed him from that position. McClellan did not support the idea of forcing abolition on all of the states. A loss to McClellan would also be a loss to the cause.

> *I am going to be beaten, and unless some great change takes place badly beaten.*
>
> —Abraham Lincoln, speaking to an army officer about his chances for reelection

In the early fall, the Union forces made many advances in the war. Their progress stirred hopes in the North for a Union victory. It also rallied support for Lincoln. In addition, many states passed laws allowing soldiers to cast **absentee** votes. Union generals gave leave to soldiers from states that did not allow absentee voting. They knew the soldiers would likely support Lincoln's stand on unconditional surrender.

On November 8, 1864, President Lincoln was elected to a second term. He won the popular vote by half a million votes. He won in all but three states: Kentucky, Delaware, and New Jersey. The election benefited other Republicans also. They gained a three-fourths majority in Congress. This meant African-American suffrage was now a possibility.

A Message of Compromise

On December 6, 1864, Lincoln sent Congress a message. He was ready to compromise on some of the issues that divided them. He was ready to accept harsher rules for Reconstruction.

As the war came to an end, many Americans believed that African-American soldiers who had fought for the Union deserved the right to vote. This picture shows the 4th U.S. Colored Infantry Division at Fort Lincoln.

The message led to more meetings between Congress and the president. Congress agreed to accept the elected representatives from Louisiana and Arkansas. In exchange, Lincoln agreed to sign a bill similar to the Wade-Davis Bill. It would set how the rest of the Confederate states could rejoin the Union. Congress wanted to give full rights of citizenship, including voting, to all African-American men. Lincoln convinced them to limit this. He thought it should only start with African-American soldiers who fought for the Union.

The Democrats were weaker in Congress, but they were not without power. They voted with Moderates to defeat the Radical versions of the bill. They voted down the Conservative versions of the bill by siding with the Radical Republicans. In the end, no bill passed.

The Democrats also were able to block the Louisiana and Arkansas representatives and senators. They voted with the Radical Republicans to keep them out of Congress. This greatly weakened those state governments.

The President Is Assassinated

With the elections behind him, Lincoln was ready for his second term. His first goal was in sight. He wanted the Thirteenth Amendment passed. The Senate had already voted in favor, but the amendment had failed to get the needed votes in the House of Representatives. He knew the amendment could easily pass when the new Republican members joined Congress. Lincoln wanted members of both parties, however, to work together to pass the amendment.

The Thirteenth Amendment Passes

Lincoln and his Secretary of State, William Seward, began **lobbying** the **lame duck** Democrats. These men would soon be out of a job and so had less reason to vote the party line. When the amendment came up for vote again in the House, 16 Democrats voted in favor. Another eight Democrats chose to be absent for the vote. On January 31, 1865, the Thirteenth Amendment was passed by Congress. Cheers rang out in the House when the amendment passed. The Republicans were overjoyed. Their cheers were echoed in the gallery, where many freedmen had gathered for the vote. Outside, loud booms filled Washington, DC. A one-hundred-gun salute with cannons was set off in honor of the event.

Major Events

1865

January 31
Thirteenth Amendment passes

March
Freedmen's Bureau established

April 9
Lee surrenders

April 11
Lincoln's last speech

April 14
Lincoln is assassinated

May 29
Johnson announces his Reconstruction plan

1866

April 9
Congress passes Civil Rights Act

27

HARPER'S WEEKLY.
A
JOURNAL OF CIVILIZATION.

Vol. IX.—No. 425.] NEW YORK, SATURDAY, FEBRUARY 18, 1865. [SINGLE COPIES TEN CENTS. $4.00 PER YEAR IN ADVANCE.

Scene in the House of Representatives upon the passage of the Thirteenth Amendment

The States Approve

After Congress passes an amendment, the states must ratify it. Within a week, eight states had approved the amendment. During the next two months, another 11 states ratified it. In the end, only three states in the North failed to approve it: Kentucky, Delaware, and New Jersey.

Lincoln always said that secession was illegal. He said the amendment needed to be approved by two-thirds of all the states because of this. This included the rebel states. Louisiana, Tennessee, and Arkansas ratified the amendment.

An End or a Beginning?

As the Thirteenth Amendment moved through the states, abolitionists broke into groups. One group felt their work was done. All slaves would be free in all states. There was nothing left to do. The other group saw that the amendment opened up a new set of questions. The slaves would be free, but what rights would they have? Where would they live? What would they do? This group knew the fight was not over. The question that had haunted the Republican Party for years was still unanswered: Would the freedmen be allowed to vote?

Dr. John Rock

It took many months to ratify the amendment and still many questions were unanswered. Change began, however, the day Congress passed the amendment.

John Rock went to medical school in Philadelphia. While practicing medicine, he studied law. He became a member of the Massachusetts State Bar. Charles Sumner, a senator from that state, brought Rock to the Supreme Court on February 1, the day after the amendment passed. Sumner wanted Rock admitted to the court for the practice of law.

> *The one question of the age is settled.*
>
> —Anti-slavery Congressman, Cornelius Cole

In 1857, the Supreme Court had ruled in the *Dred Scott* case. In that case, they had decided that African Americans were not citizens and therefore could not be heard in the courts. Three members of the Supreme Court who heard that case were still on the court. The court, however, admitted Rock into the practice of law. Chief Justice Salmon P. Chase swore him in. Rock was the first African-American man accredited to the highest court in the nation.

> *What is freedom? Is it a bare privilege of not being chained? If this is all, then freedom is a bitter mockery, a cruel delusion.*
>
> —James A. Garfield

More Changes

Freedom meant challenges for the former slaves, but it also meant opportunity. They now had choices to make. For some, this meant getting married. For others, it meant searching for family members. The sale of slaves had often torn apart families, children from parents, husbands from wives, and siblings from brothers and sisters.

In the North, the amendment also led to new state laws. African Americans were now allowed to be witnesses in federal courts. African-American men were allowed to carry mail. In some cities, such as Washington, DC, streetcars were desegregated.

Freedmen's school, Edisto Island, South Carolina

The Freedmen's Bureau

The government established the Freedmen's Bureau in March 1865 to help former slaves adjust to freedom. The Bureau was only supposed to exist for one year. It provided medical care, clothing, food, and fuel to needy freedmen and their families. As slaves, most had received no education and could not read or write. The Freedmen's Bureau established schools and sent teachers.

Once freed, many former slaves moved to cities. Jobs available to them, however, were still mainly in the countryside. The Bureau helped by providing transportation to where work was available. The Bureau also helped the freedmen get fair wages for their work.

People After the War

General Oliver Otis Howard

General O.O. Howard was the first commissioner of the Freedmen's Bureau. He believed education was the path toward improving the lives of the freed people. Under his lead, the Bureau opened schools throughout the South.

After leaving the Bureau, Howard became the president of Howard University. The college was founded to educate African Americans to become professionals, such as teachers, lawyers, doctors, and dentists.

The War Winds Down

By late March, Union forces had control of Charleston, South Carolina. The city celebrated the Union victory with a parade. Nearly 4,000 African Americans walked beside soldiers, fire companies, and tradesmen. Children carried a banner. It read, "We Know No Master But Ourselves."

On April 3, Union General Grant's troops occupied Richmond, Virginia. The Union victory was celebrated by African Americans singing, dancing, and praying in the streets.

Grant's victorious troops followed Lee's men in their retreat from Petersburg to Appomattox, Virginia. Grant offered generous surrender terms: a pardon for all soldiers. On April 9, Grant accepted Lee's surrender.

With this agreement, Grant set the terms for surrender for the rest of the Confederate troops. It was a signal that the war was ending.

Lincoln's Last Speech

On April 11, 1865, President Lincoln stood on the balcony of the White House. He spoke to the crowd gathered below. Lincoln talked about the need to rebuild the South. He promised a new plan for Reconstruction was coming soon. He also did something that no other American president had done before. He publicly supported limited African-American suffrage.

> *That is the last speech he will ever make.*
>
> —John Wilkes Booth to a companion in the crowd, April 11, 1865

The President Is Shot!

In the evening of April 14, 1865, President and Mrs. Lincoln went to Ford's Theatre in Washington, DC. As they sat watching the play, *Our American Cousin*, John Wilkes Booth entered their private box. He shot Lincoln in the back of the head. Then Booth jumped onto the stage and ran from the theater. He escaped on horseback to Virginia.

As the country mourned the loss, the army hunted for the shooter. He was found 12 days later, hiding in a barn near Port Royal, Virginia. Booth refused to surrender. The troops shot and killed him.

The soldiers did not believe Booth had worked alone. They rounded up a small group of his associates. They accused them of plotting to kill several government officials. A military court convicted the other eight members of the group. Four of them were hanged. The others were sentenced to prison and hard labor. Booth's quick death and the fast trials of the other eight left many questions unanswered.

President Lincoln's funeral procession on Pennsylvania Avenue, Washington, DC.

Presidential Reconstruction

Lincoln's death left many issues unsolved. The Thirteenth Amendment had still not been ratified. African-American suffrage was far from being settled. Despite efforts to compromise, the president and Congress had not agreed upon a new plan for states to return to the Union.

After Lincoln's death, Lincoln's vice-president, Andrew Johnson, became president. The last of the Confederate troops surrendered during Johnson's first weeks in office. Johnson announced his plan for Reconstruction, known as Presidential Reconstruction, in two proclamations on May 29, 1865. He described his plan as an attempt to carry out Lincoln's policies, however, Johnson's Presidential Reconstruction was different from Lincoln's Wartime Reconstruction in several ways.

One part of the agreement was that when former rebels signed the oath of loyalty to the Union, they regained all of their property, except for slaves. The army had already broken up former plantations and given plots of land to the freedmen. Once former rebels took the oath, the land had to be given back to them.

Johnson's plan offered amnesty and pardon to former rebels. Johnson excluded 14 groups of Southerners from the general amnesty. These groups included Confederate officials, high ranking Confederate officers, and owners of taxable property worth $20,000 (worth about $275,000 today) or more. Anyone in those 14 classes had to apply to the president for an individual pardon.

Johnson agreed with Lincoln that secession was illegal. He wanted the states to regain their place in the Union quickly. He generally followed the Ten Percent Plan; however, he did make some changes. Johnson's changes were that states had to ratify the Thirteenth Amendment and **repeal** secession. Any person who met a state's qualifications for voting before secession could vote for delegates to the state constitutional convention, except those who had not been pardoned.

President Andrew Johnson struggled with Radical Republicans over Reconstruction.

The Plan in Action

Within a few months, all of the Confederate states, except Texas, held conventions. Constitutions were written and officials were elected. Some states were able to rejoin even though they did not follow all of the rules. For example, Mississippi rejoined the Union but failed to ratify the Thirteenth Amendment.

Johnson seemed to give pardons without regard for what part the person played in the Confederacy. He granted hundreds of pardons each day. By 1866, Johnson had handed out 7,000 pardons. The pardoned included 58 men who had served in the Confederate Congress. It also included 16 men who had been in the Confederate Cabinet, and 4 generals who had fought against the Union in the war.

Many of these men became elected officials again after being pardoned. This angered the Radical Republicans and the former slaves. They knew these leaders would find ways to keep the freedmen from

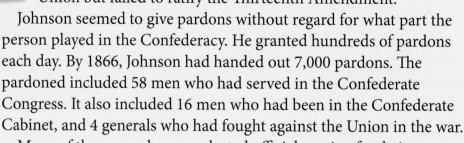

For the present, and so long as there are living witnesses of the great war of sections, there will be people who will not be consoled for the loss of a cause which they believed to be holy. As time passes, people, even of the South, will begin to wonder how it was possible that their ancestors ever fought for or justified institutions which acknowledged the right of property in man.

—Ulysses S. Grant, The Personal Memoirs of Ulysses S. Grant, 1885 enjoying their civil rights. These former Confederate officials went to Washington DC. to take their seats in Congress in December 1865. Congress refused to seat them.

Black Codes

The Southern states found many ways to keep the former slaves from claiming their rights. Each state wrote a set of laws called the **Black Codes**. On the surface, it looked as though they were giving African Americans their rights. The codes allowed African Americans to marry, own property, make contracts, and sue and be sued. The laws also allowed them to testify in the courts.

In reality, the codes put restrictions on African Americans. They could marry, but only within their race. They could testify, but only in cases that involved other African Americans. For every give, there was a take.

In addition, some states made laws that were clearly meant to return African Americans to near-slave conditions. In many states, the Black Codes allowed judges to make children apprentices of their former owners. If the child was an orphan or if the judge decided the child's parents could not support the child, the judge could send the child to work without pay.

After emancipation, many female African Americans left their jobs in the fields. The Black Codes allowed landowners to make contracts with freedmen that forced the whole family back to work in the fields.

In Mississippi, freedmen had to sign a yearly contract with their employer. If the worker quit before the year was up, he had to return all of the money he had earned that year. He could be arrested by any white man and returned to the plantation owner.

Many states also had **vagrancy** laws. These laws said a freedman without a job could be arrested and fined. If he couldn't pay the fine, the court would hire him out.

> *Things was hurt by Mr. Lincoln gettin' kilt.*
>
> —a freedman

Under Black Codes (unfair Southern laws), a black man who did not have a job could be fined. If he could not pay the fine, his services could be sold to the highest bidder, as shown here.

> " *Slavery is not abolished until the black man has the ballot.*
>
> —Frederick Douglass "

Some states made fence laws only in African-American counties to keep the freedmen from owning livestock. In South Carolina, African Americans had to pay an annual tax if they wanted to work as anything other than a farmer or a servant. All of these laws made it easy to arrest a freedman. Then he was at the mercy of an all-white court system.

The Black Codes angered both the Moderate and Radical Republicans. They wanted a new plan to protect the rights of African Americans.

The Civil Rights Act of 1866

Congress wanted to end the Black Codes and stop the violence against African Americans that was spreading across the South. It took two major steps to reach those goals. The first was to pass an act to keep and enlarge the Freedmen's Bureau. The bureau had done much to help African Americans, but there was much more to be done. The second was to pass the Civil Rights Act. The act gave citizenship to African Americans. As citizens, they could make and enforce contracts, sue, and give evidence in court. The people could inherit, purchase, lease, sell, hold, and **convey** real and personal property. The act gave equal benefits of all laws to African Americans. It also made it illegal for states to pass Black Codes. Anyone caught interfering with these rights could be arrested, fined up to $1,000, and jailed for up to a year. Once again, though, it fell short of giving African Americans the right to vote.

Johnson Responds

The president vetoed both acts. He said the Constitution did not give Congress these powers. This angered Moderate Republicans who had been working to improve Johnson's plan. It also angered Radical Republicans. They saw Johnson as supporting Southern attempts to keep African Americans in slave-like conditions.

The vetoes signaled the end of Presidential Reconstruction. Congress was no longer willing to support Johnson's approach to rebuilding the nation.

What Do You Know!

The saying, "Your name is mud!" means that person is thought poorly of. Many people think that this phrase started with Dr. Samuel Mudd, a man who conspired to assassinate Lincoln, but people actually used it long before Lincoln's assassination.

Aftermath of the War

The results of the last congressional elections meant the Republicans were not only angry, they were powerful too. They had enough votes to override Johnson's vetoes. The Civil Rights Act became law. The Freedman's Bureau was continued. The divide between the president and Congress became too deep to mend.

The Freedmen's Bureau and many private organizations helped the country adjust to life after the war. In the North, this was much easier than in the South. Most of the fighting and destruction had taken place in Southern states. More than one-fifth of the Southern white men died during the war. In addition, Southern economic and social structures were shattered. Many Northerners felt it was their duty to rebuild the South.

Coming Home

Union soldiers returned home with about $250 in final pay (worth about $3,400 today) and a government pension. Organizations such as the Grand Army of the Republic (GAR) were formed. The GAR included men who had served for the Union during the Civil War. It provided social connections and looked after members' needs.

Major Events

1865

May
Civil War ends
Jefferson Davis captured

1866

June
Congress passes Fourteenth Amendment

1867

March
Reconstruction Acts passed

August
Johnson impeached

1868

June
Six Southern states rejoin the Union

1869

July
Fourteenth Amendment adopted

1870

February
Fifteenth Amendment adopted

July
Last three Southern states rejoin the Union

1877

April
Reconstruction ends

Former Confederate soldiers had less help. They did not receive final pay, and the money they had earned during the war was in worthless Confederate dollars. In addition, these soldiers did not receive government pensions until after Reconstruction ended.

A Strong Northern Economy

During the war, the demand for industrial and farm products was met by Northerners. Factories were opened and the railroads were expanded. Jobs were plentiful. Large companies and individual businessmen prospered. In addition, without Southern representatives in Congress, the government was able to pass taxes, tariffs, and laws that benefited Northern businesses.

A Broken Southern Economy

In the South, there was little left to the economy. Personal wealth, which had once been largely measured in slaves, had vanished. In one county in Alabama, the average wealth among whites was $18,000 in 1860 (worth over $200,000 today). By 1870, it had dropped to $3,000 (worth about $40,000 today). The physical damage to the South was vast. Hunger and disease were common. The cost to address these problems was huge. Emancipation threatened the plantation economy. Many Southern whites felt their states had lost their identity. They believed the myth of the "Lost Cause." In other words, they thought their noble culture had been destroyed by outsiders.

> *If the [Emancipation] Proclamation makes the slaves actually free, there will come the further duty of making them work...*
>
> —*New York Times*, January 1863

The Fourteenth Amendment

While the South faced the task of rebuilding, Congress acted to protect the rights of the freedmen. Members of Congress worried about Johnson's next move. They thought their override of the president's vetoes might be challenged in the courts. Congress thought another amendment was the answer to its problems.

The Fourteenth Amendment gave full citizenship to all people born in the United States, except for Native Americans. It said no state could block citizens from their rights. It also said states had to give every citizen "equal protection under the laws."

The amendment did another important thing. It said the Union was not responsible for the Confederate debts. The Union would not "buy" the freedom of the African Americans from their former owners.

If a state blocked a male citizen from voting, it faced punishment. It could lose some voting privileges in Congress. At the same time, the amendment took some powers away from the president. The amendment proposed a new plan to deal with former Confederate leaders. It said they could not hold public office unless they had a pardon from Congress. A congressional pardon required a two-thirds majority vote. President Johnson could no longer pass out pardons on his own.

The Fourteenth Amendment was adopted in 1868. With the Fourteenth Amendment, Congress took charge of Reconstruction. The Republicans had a two-thirds majority and Johnson was powerless to stop them. He knew they could override any veto. The period known as Radical Reconstruction had begun.

Reaction to the Amendment

Johnson campaigned against members of his own party running for Congress. He wanted to remove the power the Radicals had over him. As Johnson fought against his fellow Republicans, two major riots broke out in the South.

On May 1, 1866, in Memphis, Tennessee, a fight broke out between a group of African-American Union soldiers and local police. A wave of violence lasted for three days. Three months later, another race riot began in New Orleans, Louisiana. By the time it was over, 34 African Americans and 3 white Republicans had been killed.

People After the War

Hiram Revels

Hiram Revels, U.S. senator from Mississippi, was the first African American elected to the Senate. He argued against segregation and worked for civil rights. Before joining the Senate in 1870, Revels had recruited African Americans for the Union army and opened a freedmen's school.

> *Wherever I go—the street, the shop, the hotel, or the steamboat—I hear the people talk in such a way as to indicate they are yet unable to conceive of the Negro as possessing any rights at all.*
>
> —Carl Schurz, after touring the South

Northerners were outraged. Growing violence in the South made them feel more certain the federal government needed to take control of the South. This increased support for the Radical Republicans and their plan.

The Reconstruction Acts

On March 2, 1867, Congress passed its first Reconstruction Act. It included seven main provisions:

1. New governments were formed in the ten states that did not ratify the Fourteenth Amendment.
2. Ten states that did not ratify the amendment were divided into five military districts. Each district was under the authority of a military commander.
3. Tennessee was readmitted to the Union.
4. African Americans could vote in state elections.
5. Former Confederate leaders could not hold office.
6. States had to ratify the Fourteenth Amendment for readmission.
7. States had to submit their new constitutions to Congress for approval.

The second Reconstruction Act was passed a few weeks later. It required the military to register voters and help the state prepare for a convention. Congress passed two other Reconstruction Acts.

Johnson criticized these acts. He said the military should not replace Southern officials. Congress responded by passing another act. This one said the military government took precedence over governments elected under Presidential Reconstruction.

Congress responded to conflict with the president by passing more acts. As commander-in-chief, the president could tell the military governors what to do. The Tenure of Office Act of March, 1867 was a direct attack on presidential powers. It said the president could not remove government officials, including members of his own Cabinet, without approval from the Senate.

Johnson Responds

That summer Johnson decided to act while Congress was not in session. He suspended his Secretary of War, Edwin Stanton. When the Senate met again, they refused to approve the suspension.

Johnson fought back by removing Stanton from his Cabinet. He also appointed new military commanders in some of the districts. He chose generals the Radicals would not approve.

Impeachment

Congress would not accept this behavior. The House voted to **impeach** the president. Impeach means to formally charge with wrongdoing. They sent Johnson's case to the Senate for trial.

The trial began on March 4, 1868. It lasted three months. His defenders said Johnson was acting within his powers. They said he had a right to challenge laws he believed were against the Constitution. They also said that Johnson had not acted against the Tenure of Office Act, because the Act only applied to people Johnson had appointed. Stanton had been appointed by Lincoln. In May, the Senate voted but fell one vote short of the required two-thirds majority needed to impeach the president. On May 26, the Senate dropped the case.

Southern Military Districts, 1867

What Do You Know!

State constitutional conventions often broke down in chaos. In Florida, the lieutenant governor grabbed the state seal and claimed his right to rule the state.

Amnesty for Davis

There had been much debate about what charges to bring against Jefferson Davis, the leader of the Confederacy. The government finally charged him with treason. Davis demanded a trial, hoping to use it to make a case for secession.

The government asked for several delays to prepare for the trial. When Davis went to court, his defenders argued that the Fourteenth Amendment had already punished him. That law said he could not run for public office. They said giving him further punishment would go against the double jeopardy rule of the Fifth Amendment. The court was divided. Before a decision could be made, President Johnson signed the Amnesty Proclamation on December 25, 1868. This pardoned everyone who fought in the rebellion, including Davis.

The Nation Is Restored

The Reconstruction Acts led to hundreds of thousands of African Americans becoming voters. Most of them voted with the Republicans. It also led to many white Southern men staying away from the polls. They declined to take part in an election if that meant participating with African Americans.

The African-American vote helped elect Republican General Ulysses S. Grant president in 1868. It also helped Republicans gain control of Southern state governments. In turn, seven states were ready for readmission by 1868: Alabama, Arkansas, Florida, Georgia, Louisiana, North Carolina, and South Carolina. By 1870, Mississippi, Virginia, and Texas were also readmitted.

> *The war is over; the South is conquered; I have no longer any country but America, and it is for the honor of America, as for my own honor and life, that I plead against this degradation. Kill me! Kill me rather than inflict on me, and on my people through me, this insult worse than death.*
>
> —Jefferson Davis, May 23, 1865, protesting his treatment

African-American Leaders

In some areas, African-American voters outnumbered white voters. In these places, African Americans held leadership roles in local government. They also began taking their place in state and national government. Between 1869 and 1880, 16 African Americans served in the House of Representatives and two served in the Senate.

Ku Klux Klan

Congress could not stop the flow of hatred with acts and amendments. Southern states found ways around these mandates. In reality, most African Americans had very little power. Gangs of white men were free to terrorize them.

Some violence came from poor whites' fear of losing what economic stability they had achieved. Some of the violence was meant to keep African Americans from voting. Some people acted alone, while others organized into groups. The most well-known group was the Ku Klux Klan.

The Klan started in Tennessee in late 1865 or early 1866. It was formed as a social group. By 1867, the Klan had groups throughout the South. Nathan Bedford Forrest was its Grand Wizard. Forrest had been a slave trader, a cotton plantation owner, and had been a general in the Confederate army. The Klan worked to end Republican rule in the South and restore a system of white supremacy.

The Klan used violence and scare tactics to meet its goals. Its victims were African Americans and white Republicans. The Klan burned down African-American churches, schools, and homes. Klan members would make midnight raids. They would take African Americans from their homes and whip or hang them. Members wore white hoods and sheets to hide their identities. Authorities rarely interfered with their activities. Some authorities supported the Klan's actions. Others feared the Klan.

Klan activity rose around election times. Republicans (white and African American) would be killed as a warning for others to stay away from the polls. Republicans began losing power in Southern states.

This cartoon, critical of the Grant administration, shows a woman, the "Solid South," carrying President Grant in a carpet bag. "Carpetbaggers" were corrupt Republican appointees in the South who were resented by many Southern whites.

> "[He was] too big a man... he could write and read and put it down himself.
>
> —brother of Washington Eager, on why the Klan killed Eager"

This cartoon entitled "Worse than Slavery" shows harassment of African Americans by the White League (left) and the Ku Klux Klan.

Controlling Klan violence was difficult. Governors of Tennessee, Arkansas, and Texas had the most success.

Congress passed a series of Enforcement Acts. The third act is known as the Ku Klux Klan Act. This law made the Klan's scare tactics and violence a federal crime. If states did not uphold the law, then federal courts would handle the cases. This helped decrease violence in the South. President Grant was reelected in 1872, partly through the support of the South. The acts had allowed a fair election where everyone's vote counted. The law slowed the violence, but it didn't end it completely.

The Fifteenth Amendment

The last major piece of Reconstruction legislation was the Fifteenth Amendment. Passed in February 1869, the bill said that neither state nor federal government could keep any male from voting based on race, color, or previous condition of servitude. It was ratified the next year. African-American men had won the right to vote in every state and American territory.

Reconstruction Ends

Northerners had been willing to help the South rebuild while the Northern economy was doing well. In 1873, however, the situation changed. Jay Cooke and Company was a major investor in the railroads. It was also the main backer of the Union war effort. The company got caught lying about the value of the land along the railroad tracks. The problem grew and the company declared bankruptcy. This started the Panic of 1873. Sellers outnumbered buyers on the stock market. Companies had to buy back their own stock.

> [The Klan] broke my door open, took me out of bed, took me to the woods and whipped me three hours or more and left me for dead. They said, 'Do you think you will ever vote another damn radical ticket?' They set in and whipped me a thousand licks more with sticks and straps that had buckles on them.
>
> —from testimony to the Joint Select Committee to inquire into the Condition of Affairs in the Late Insurrectionary States

Within two years, 89 of 364 railroads had failed. Another 18,000 businesses, including many small banks, closed. By 1876, about two million people were out of work. Those with jobs faced pay cuts. Strikes and protests broke out in the North. People were more worried about their own money problems than about the African Americans in the South.

In 1874, Democrats regained control of the House. In 1876, Rutherford B. Hayes was elected president. Although a Republican, he turned away from Reconstruction. He supported state and local control over government. He said Southerners should be allowed to handle their own problems. He removed federal troops in the South that enforced laws guaranteeing equal rights. Reconstruction was over.

The Aftermath

One of the lasting positive effects of Reconstruction was progress in education. In addition to the schools built by the Freedmen's Bureau and other social organizations, African Americans themselves established schools. Public school systems were now open to African Americans. By the 1870s, literacy rates among whites rose to 50 percent. Among African Americans, it was 40 percent. Colleges and training programs helped African Americans improve their lives.

Reconstruction, though, did little to improve the economic standing of the African Americans. Without money to buy land, many of the freedmen became sharecroppers. They rented land to farm in exchange for a portion of the crops they raised. The system left most African-American families poor.

When Democrats regained power in the 1880s, the South tried to reinvent itself. The "New South" added industries such as coal, tobacco, and lumber to its economy. Cotton mills provided jobs for white women and children. The railroad system provided ways to ship goods to ports in the North and South.

With the return of Democrats, however, state governments found new ways around laws guaranteeing African-American rights. Poll taxes (a fee to vote) and literacy tests were used to prevent African Americans from voting.

In the 1890s, many Southern states passed Jim Crow laws. These laws kept African Americans separate from whites in almost every public

People After the War

Blanche Bruce

Blanche Bruce was elected to the U.S. Senate from Mississippi in 1874. During his term, he argued against segregation in the U.S. Army and for better policies toward Native Americans. Before that, he was a runaway slave who went on to open Missouri's first school for African Americans.

place. In 1896, an African-American man refused to leave a whites-only train car. He was arrested. Later, he sued the railroad. The case, *Plessy* v. *Ferguson*, went to the Supreme Court. The court ruled in favor of the railroad. It said separate but equal treatment was legal and acceptable.

That case and later Supreme Court decisions undid much of the progress African Americans made during Reconstruction.

> " *The slave went free; stood a moment in the sun, then moved back again toward slavery.*
>
> —W.E.B. DuBois "

Violence and discrimination continued for decades.

Later Civil Rights Gains

In 1920, women were granted suffrage. The next legislation to improve civil rights came in 1948. Executive Order 9981 said that all members of the armed forces were entitled to equal treatment and opportunity. In the 1950s, progress was made breaking down segregation. The Civil Rights Act of 1964 made all kinds of discrimination illegal. In 1991, another Civil Rights Act strengthened the laws.

Reconstruction did not live up to many people's expectations. Many of the gains made during Reconstruction were lost, not to be regained until many decades later. Reconstruction was, however, an important time when the United States began to address and repair the wounds of slavery and move toward equal treatment for all.

GLOSSARY

absentee In relation to voting, a person who votes from a remote location by mail instead of at home

amnesty A pardon or forgiveness for offenses against the government

Black Codes Unfair laws enacted in Southern states after the Civil War for the purpose of returning African Americans to slave-like conditions

Conditional Unionists Southerners who still felt strong ties to the Union after the Civil War and were quick to take the oath of allegiance so their state could rejoin the Union

constitutional amendment A change to the constitution of a state or national government

contraband Escaped slaves

contradict To deny the truth of a statement by proposing an opposite point of view

convey To legally transfer the ownership of property

desegregation A plan to bring together people of different races so they live, work, and go to school together

disenfranchise To take the right to vote away from a group or individual

domestic Relating to the home and family or relating to one's own country rather than a foreign nation

emancipation Being freed from enslavement

executive branch Branch of government led by the president of the United States which is responsible for carrying out the nation's laws

franchise To give people the right to vote

impeach To formally accuse a public official of wrongdoing with the intent of removing the official from office

indestructible A person, thing, or idea that is difficult or impossible to destroy

Ironclad Unionists People in the South who did not support the Confederacy

lame duck A public official who is in office while waiting to be replaced by an elected successor

lobbying The attempt to influence a public official, such as a congressman or senator, to support legislation

manifesto A public statement of one's views or intended actions

opposition A group of people who think differently or propose a different policy or action

pocket veto A president's indirect veto of a bill by refusing to sign it within ten days of when Congress adjourns

postpone To put off until another time

preamble An introduction at the beginning of a document that explains the document's purpose

prohibited Something that is not allowed

ratify To approve

Reconstruction The period after the Civil War devoted to bringing the states that belonged to the Confederate States of America back into the Union and rebuilding them

repeal To legally rescind, or overturn, an existing law

segregate To keep apart or separate

social equality A condition within society where all people, regardless of race, religion, or background, have a similar economic and social status

suffrage The legal right to vote

supremacy The condition of being the highest in rank; superior to others

vagrancy The condition of being at loose ends, without a job, and homeless

MORE INFORMATION

Books

Bolden, Tonya. *Cause: Reconstruction America 1863–1877*. Knopf Books for Young Readers, 2005.

Elliot, Henry. *Frederick Douglass: From Slavery to Statesman*. Crabtree Publishing Company, 2010.

Greene, Meg. *Into the Land of Freedom: African Americans in Reconstruction*. Lerner Publishing Group, 2004.

Hakim, Joy. *Reconstructing America: 1865–1890*. Oxford University Press, 2007.

Peacock, Judith. *Reconstruction: Rebuilding After the Civil War*. Capstone, 2006.

Stroud, Bettye and Virginia Schomp. *The Reconstruction Era*. Benchmark Books, 2006.

Websites

www.archives.gov/research/ african-americans/freedmens-bureau/ African-American heritage page of the National Archives Website. Contains records for genealogists and social historians and information about the history of the Freedmen's Bureau.

www.digitalhistory.uh.edu/ reconstruction/index.html Photos and text relate the story of Reconstruction.

www.pbs.org/wgbh/amex/reconstruction/ PBS Website. Has text, photos, and video about Reconstruction.

http://memory.loc.gov/ammem/aaohtml/ exhibit/aopart5.html Library of Congress site on Reconstruction. Includes artwork, photos, primary sources, and facts.

http://blackhistory.harpweek.com/4Reconst ruction/ReconLevelOne.htm Harper's Weekly was published during the Civil War and Reconstruction. This site includes copies of editorials, political cartoons, and illustrations.

 About the Author

Lisa Cocca is a freelance writer and editor living and working in New Jersey.

INDEX

abolition, 5, 7–9, 13, 16, 25
African Americans, 8, 10–13, 16, 17, 20, 22, 24, 29, 30, 33, 34, 37, 38, 40–44
  economic issues of, 16, 43
  female, 33
  living conditions of, 16
  and Medal of Honor, 8
  political leaders, 16, 37, 41, 43
  soldiers, 8, 12, 16, 26
  See also suffrage, African American

Banks, Nathaniel, 13, 14, 16, 17, 19
Battle Hymn of the Republic, 9
Black Codes, 33, 34
Booth, John Wilkes, 30, 31
Brown, John, 9
Bruce, Blanche, 43
Butler, Benjamin, 16

carpetbaggers, 41
Civil Rights Act of 1866, 27, 34, 35
Civil Rights Act of 1964, 44
Cole, Cornelius, 28
Conditional Unionists, 13
Confederate
  amnesty, 8–11, 14, 17, 21, 31, 40
  army, 9, 30, 31, 36, 41
  Cabinet, 32
  Congress, 32
  debts, 37
  leaders, 8, 9, 31, 32, 37, 38
  states, 9, 17, 22, 25, 32
Congress, U.S., 6, 7, 10, 11, 17–28, 31, 32, 34–39, 41, 42
Constitution, U.S., 10, 20, 21, 23, 34, 40
contraband (former slaves), 16

Davis, Henry W., 11, 18, 22–24
Davis, Jefferson, 35, 40
Democrats, 5–7, 12, 19, 20, 25, 26, 27, 43
  lame duck, 27
  Northern 6, 7
  Southern, 5
disenfranchise, 20
District of Columbia Emancipation Act, 6
Dred Scott case, 29
Durrant, Thomas J., 13

economy
  Northern, 36, 42
  Southern, 5, 36, 43
election of 1864, 23–25
emancipation, 5, 6, 13, 16, 17, 21, 33, 36
Emancipation Proclamation, 7, 8, 15, 36

executive branch, 6, 10

Fifteenth Amendment, 35, 42
Fifth Amendment, 40
Forrest, Nathan Bedford, 41
Fourteenth Amendment, 35–38, 40
franchise, 20
freedmen, 12, 15, 16, 19, 24, 27–34
Freedmen's Bureau, 27, 29, 30, 34, 35, 43
Free State General Committee, 13

Grant, Ulysses S., 30, 32, 41, 42

Hayes, Rutherford B., 43
Houzeau, Jean-Charles, 24
Howard, Oliver O., 30

Ironclad Unionists, 19
Johnson, Andrew, 9, 12, 27, 31, 32, 34, 35, 37–40
  and Amnesty Proclamation, 40
  impeachment of, 35, 39, 40

Ku Klux Klan, 41, 42

Lincoln, Abraham, 5-14, 17–19, 20–24, 27, 28, 31–34, 40
  Reconstruction plans of, 8, 9, 11–17, 19–22, 24, 25
  See also Ten Percent Plan and election of 1864.
Lost Cause, Southern, 36
Louisiana, 11, 12–14, 17, 19, 22, 24–26, 28, 38, 39, 41
  state constitution, 13, 14, 20, 24

Military Districts, Southern, 39
Mudd, Samuel, 34

Panic of 1873, 43
Phelps, John S., 12
Plessy v. *Ferguson*, 44
presidential reconstruction plans
  of Johnson, 31–34
  of Lincoln, 8, 11–26
  See also Ten Percent Plan
Proclamation of Amnesty and Reconstruction, 1, 8, 11, 17, 18, 21

Radical Reconstruction, 17, 18, 37–42
Radical Republicans
  See Republicans, Radical
railroads, 36, 42, 43
Reconstruction Acts, 38, 40, 41

Reconstruction
  British reaction to, 8
  end of, 42
  evolution of, 5
  Johnson's plan, 31–34
  Lincoln's plan, 8, 11–26
  See also Radical Reconstruction, Ten Percent Plan
Republicans, 5, 6, 9, 10, 28, 32, 34
  Conservative, 6, 13, 26
  Moderate, 10, 26, 34
  Radical, 6, 9, 10, 13, 14, 17, 18, 20, 21, 24, 32, 34, 37–39
Revels, Hiram, 37
Richmond, Virginia, 10, 15, 30
Rock, John, 28, 29

secession, 6, 9, 10, 23, 28, 32, 40
Second Confiscation Act, 5, 7
Shepley, George F., 12, 13
slavery, 5–7, 12–16, 20, 22–24, 34, 42, 44
slaves, 5–10, 12–19, 21, 28–32, 33, 36
social equality, 8, 22, 24, 29
state constitutions, 12–14, 16, 19, 21, 22, 24, 32, 38, 39
Stevens, Thaddeus, 17, 18
suffrage
  African American, 9, 10, 13, 14, 17, 18, 20, 22–26, 30, 31, 34, 38, 40, 42, 44
  and women, 44
Sumner, Charles, 18, 29

Ten Percent Plan, 11–14, 17, 22, 32
  and Arkansas, 12
  and Louisiana, 12–14, 22
  and Mississippi, 12
  and Virginia, 12
  strengths and weaknesses of, 14–15
Thirteenth Amendment, 19–21, 23, 24, 27–29, 31, 32

vagrancy laws, 33
veto, 19, 23, 34, 35, 37
  pocket, 19, 23

Wade, Benjamin, 11, 18, 20, 21, 23, 24
Wade-Davis Bill, 11, 18, 19–26
Wade-Davis manifesto, 23

Ward, Julia, 9
Whigs, 5, 13
white supremacy, 10, 37